FUN SCIENCE

Experiments in

with Toys and Everyday Stuff

BY NATALIE ROMPELLA

Consultant:

Paul Ohmann, PhD
Associate Professor of Physics
University of St. Thomas
St. Paul, Minnesota

CAPSTONE PRESS
a capstone imprint

First Facts are published by Capstone Press,
1710 Roe Crest Drive, North Mankato, Minnesota 56003
www.capstonepub.com

Library of Congress Cataloging-in-Publication Data
Rompella, Natalie, author.
  Experiments in material and matter with toys and everyday stuff / by Natalie Rompella.
      pages cm.—(First facts. Fun science)
  Includes bibliographical references and index.
  Summary: "Step-by-step instructions for experiments pertaining to material and matter"—Provided by publisher.
  Audience: 5–8.
  Audience: K to 3.
  ISBN 978-1-4914-5034-5 (library binding)
  ISBN 978-1-4914-5074-1 (paperback)
  ISBN 978-1-4914-5078-9 (eBook PDF)
  1. Matter—Properties—Experiments—Juvenile literature. I. Title. II. Series: First facts. Fun science
  QC173.16.R66 2016
  530.078—dc23   2014044898

Editorial Credits
Alesha Sullivan, editor; Kyle Grenz, designer; Jo Miller, media researcher;
Kathy McColley, production specialist

Printed in the United States   6571

TABLE OF CONTENTS

TURN YOUR HOME INTO A SCIENCE LAB!

Our world is made up of **matter**. It makes up everything from a basketball to a lollipop to a crayon. Matter comes in three forms: **liquid**, **solid**, and **gas**.

Examples of liquids:
water, shampoo, lava from a volcano

Examples of solids:
books, rocks, ice

Examples of gases:
steam from a hot cup of coffee, stinky smell left behind after a skunk sprays, air inside of a blown-up balloon

matter—anything that has weight and takes up space
liquid—matter that is wet and can be poured, such as water
solid—matter that holds its shape
gas—matter that is not solid or liquid; a gas can move about freely and does not have a definite shape

We drink matter, breathe matter, and best of all, we play with matter. You can learn all about matter through fun experiments. All you need are some toys and objects you already own!

Safety First!

You may need an adult's help for some of these experiments. But most of them can be done on your own. If you have a question about how to do a step safely, be sure to ask an adult. Think safety first!

FLIP TO PAGE 20 TO SEE HOW THE SCIENCE WORKS IN EACH EXPERIMENT!

VEHICLE WEIGH STATION

Matter has weight. Sometimes it's important to know the weight of objects. Fruits and vegetables are weighed at the grocery store. Semitrucks are weighed on the highway to be sure they aren't too heavy. Create your own **balance scale** to weigh your toy cars and trucks!

Materials:

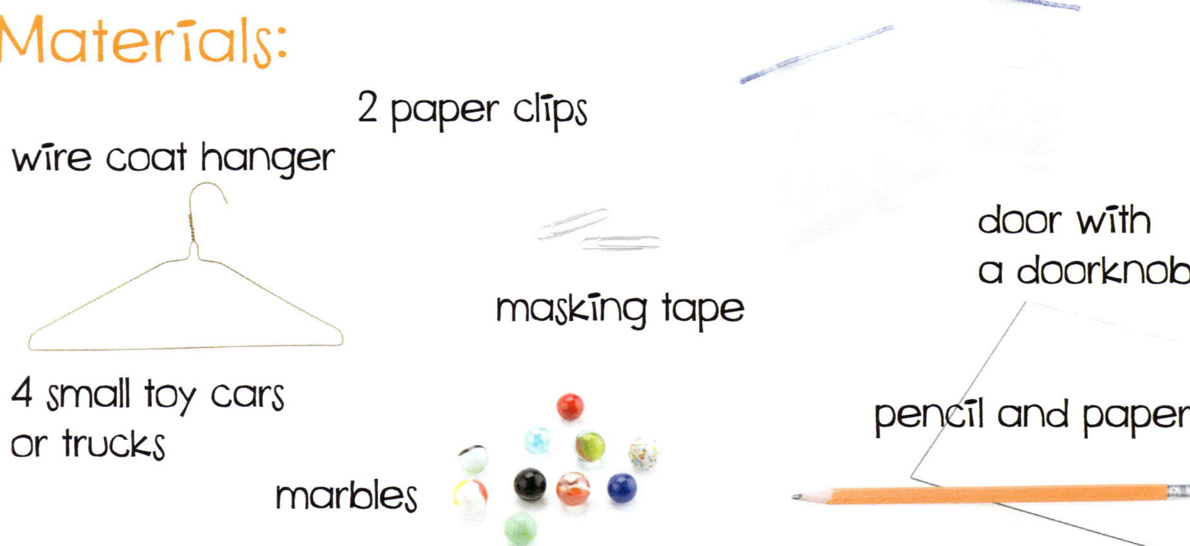

balance scale—an instrument used for weighing things; when two objects are balanced, they weigh the same

Steps:

1. **Create a balance scale by bending open the paper clips so they are in the shape of an "S." Hook them around the bottom corners of a coat hanger. Tape into place.**

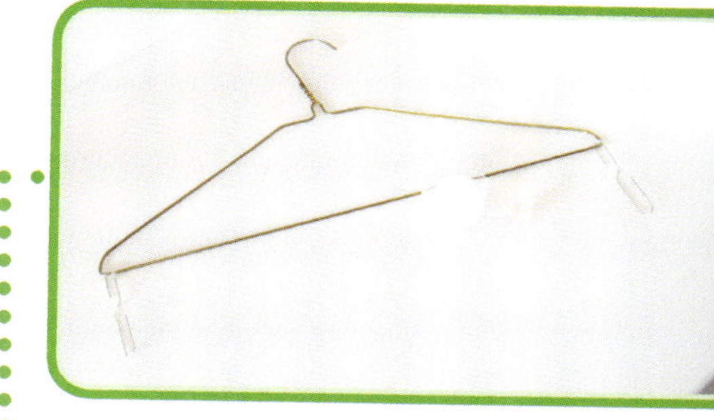

2. **Connect a bag to the open end of one of the paper clips by poking the top through the paper clip. Be sure the bag can open. Do the same on the other side of the hanger.**

3. **Hang your scale on a doorknob.**

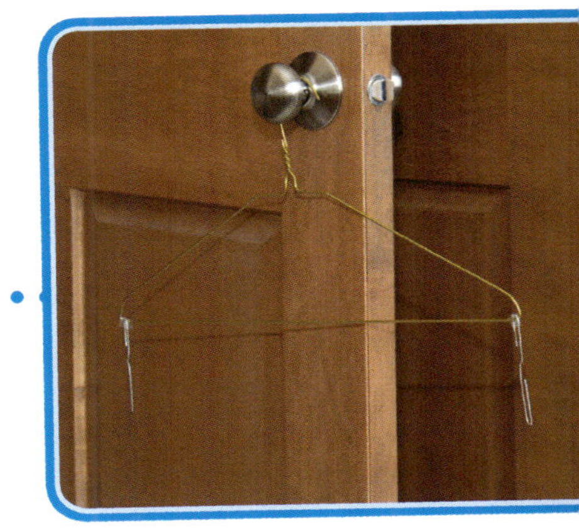

4. **Place one toy car inside the bag on one side of the scale. Add marbles slowly to the other side until the scale is even. Write down how many marbles you used to balance the two sides.**

5. **Repeat these steps for the other cars or toys. Which of your toys was the heaviest? Were there any that balanced using the same number of marbles?**

THAT'S A SINKER!

Matter can do all sorts of fun things. Some types of matter stick to a magnet. Some can bend, such as rubber. Some matter **floats** in a liquid. However it can be hard to guess what will happen to an object in water. Do you have toys that you think will sink or float in water?

Materials:

Ask an adult to help you choose 8 to 10 toys that are able to get wet

sink or large container of water

Tip:

Be sure not to use any battery-operated or electronic toys.

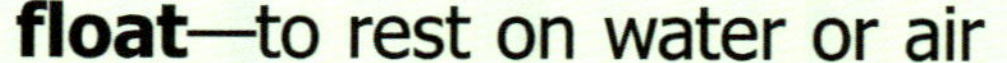

float—to rest on water or air

Steps:

1. Sort the toys you think will sink and the toys you think will float.

2. Fill your sink or a large container with water.

3. One by one, set each toy in the water. Which sank and which floated? Were your guesses right? What do you think made some toys float and some toys sink?

GAS-POWERED CAR

You might think you can see all types of matter. But we often can't see gas. Gas does not have a shape, and it can move freely. Oxygen that we breathe is a gas. Do you think you could use gas in a balloon to power one of your toy cars? Give it a try!

Materials:

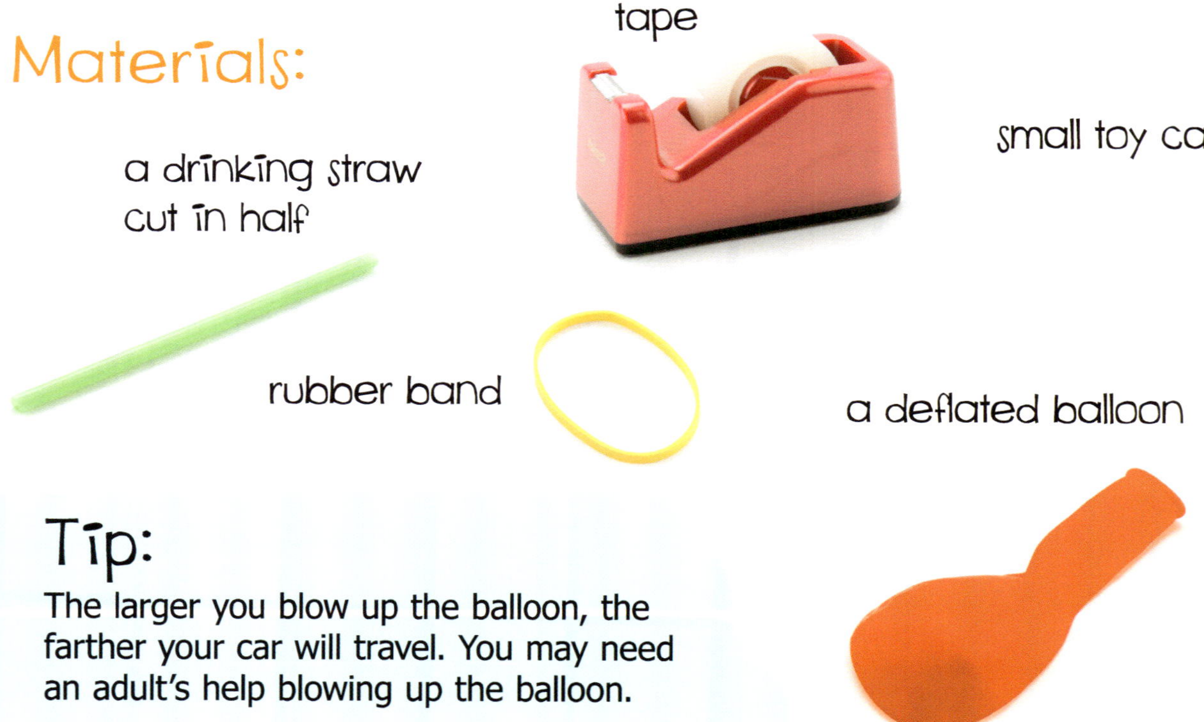

Tip:

The larger you blow up the balloon, the farther your car will travel. You may need an adult's help blowing up the balloon.

Steps:

1. **Place the end of the straw inside the opening of the balloon. Secure the balloon's opening tightly with the rubber band.**

2. **Tape the middle of the straw to the top of the car, near the front. Leave enough space on the other end of the straw so you can blow into it.**

3. **Blow up the balloon and hold the end of the straw closed with your finger.**

4. **Set the car on the ground and let go of the end of the straw. Did your car move forward?**

Fact:

Gas can also move really large objects, such as hot air balloons. The first hot air balloon took flight in 1783 in Paris, France.

DRY THOSE CLOTHES!

Have you ever noticed how a drinking glass gets beads of water on the outside of it when a room is warm? This process is called **condensation**. Or on a hot day, has your wet swimsuit ever dried on its own? The water in your swimsuit disappeared because of **evaporation**. In this easy experiment, you can see both in action!

Materials:

water

doll clothes, a sock, or a washcloth

empty plastic container with a clear lid

condensation—to change from a gas to a liquid
evaporation—to change from a liquid to a gas

Steps:

1. Wet the piece of clothing. Place it in the plastic container, and shut the lid.

2. Set the container in the sun for 2 to 3 hours.

3. Look at the lid. What happened inside the container? How do you think that happened?

Tip:

If you can't go outside, set the container by a window or in a warm room.

EGG-SPLOSION

Water is a powerful force, especially when it **freezes**. Water that gets into cracks in a road and then freezes can cause the road to split apart. See how powerful water can be when it changes from a liquid to a solid using a few simple supplies!

Materials:

plastic egg

small, plastic re-sealable bag

bowl of water

Tip:

Never put something in the freezer that could explode or shatter, such as a glass container.

freeze—to become solid or icy at a very low temperature

Steps:

1. If there are holes in the ends of the plastic egg, cover them with tape. Open the plastic egg. Submerge the egg in the bowl of water until it is full of water, and then shut the egg.

2. Place the egg in a plastic bag in case it leaks.

3. Freeze for 4 to 5 hours.

4. Check the egg. What happened to the water inside the egg?

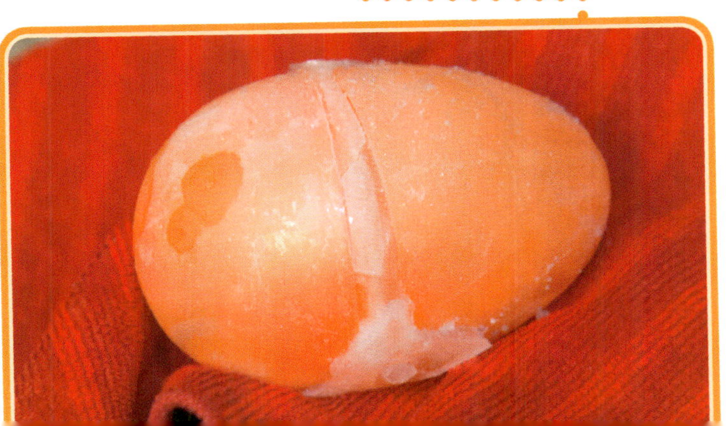

MELTING MATTER

Your toys are all made from different kinds of matter. Some toy cars are made from metal. Interlocking toy bricks are made from plastic. Crayons are made of wax. Metal, plastic, and wax can all be **melted** down and poured into a **mold** to make objects we use every day. Try making new crayons by melting down your old ones!

oven foil baking cups

Materials:

potholders

old muffin tin

paper

old or broken crayons

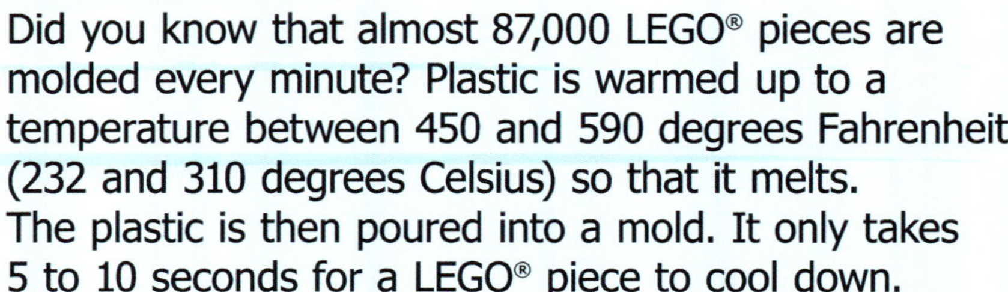

Did you know that almost 87,000 LEGO® pieces are molded every minute? Plastic is warmed up to a temperature between 450 and 590 degrees Fahrenheit (232 and 310 degrees Celsius) so that it melts.
The plastic is then poured into a mold. It only takes 5 to 10 seconds for a LEGO® piece to cool down.

Steps:

1. **Ask an adult to pre-heat the oven to 225° F (107° C).**

2. **Line the cups in the muffin tin with foil baking cups.**

3. **Remove the wrappers from old or broken crayons. Break the crayons into smaller pieces.**

4. **Place crayons in the muffin tin until they are halfway full.**

5. **Ask an adult to place the tin in the oven. Leave it in the oven for 10 minutes or until the crayons are completely melted. Have an adult remove the tin from the oven. Let cool.**

6. **Remove the molded crayons from the foil baking cups. Color away!**

melt—to change from a solid to a liquid
mold—a model of an object

WHAT'S THE MATTER WITH THIS MATTER?

If liquids flow and solids hold a shape, is jelly a solid or a liquid? What about whipped cream? Not all matter is easy to call a solid, liquid, or gas. See if you can figure out what type of matter this mystery **mixture** is!

Materials:

piece of cardboard

spoon

¼ cup (59 mL) cornstarch

2 tablespoons (30 mL) water (green food coloring optional)

small ball

toy car

toy hammer

shallow pie pan

mixture—something made up of different things mixed together

Steps:

1. Lay out a piece of cardboard on your work space.

2. Using a spoon, mix together the cornstarch and water in a shallow pie pan and stir. Be sure to get all the way to the bottom. Is the mixture a solid or a liquid?

3. Set a toy car on the mixture. Does the car sink or stay above the surface? Now drive the car through it. Does it sink or stay above the surface?

4. Hit the mixture with a toy hammer. Does it splash like a liquid?

5. Try bouncing a ball on the surface. Does it bounce? Would you say this mixture is a solid or a liquid?

Tip:

When you are done with your mixture, throw it away. Do not dump it in a sink. The water and cornstarch will eventually separate, and the cornstarch could clog the drain.

WHY IT WORKS

Are you wondering how these amazing experiments worked? Here is the science behind the fun!

PAGE 6 - VEHICLE WEIGH STATION

The balance scale compared objects with another weight, such as the marbles. If the side with the object was lower than the side with the marbles, it weighed more than the marbles. If the side with the object was higher than the side with the marbles, it weighed less. When the two sides of a scale were equal, it means the object weighed the same as the marbles.

PAGE 8 - THAT'S A SINKER!

An object will float or sink depending on its weight and size. This is called its **density**. If the object was denser than water, it sank. If it was less dense than water, it floated.

PAGE 10 - GAS-POWERED CAR

Because the balloon isn't tied shut, the air inside (which is a gas) pushed out of the balloon. The rushing air caused the toy car to move.

PAGE 12 - DRY THOSE CLOTHES!

As the water in the container heated in the Sun, it turned into **water vapor**. The vapor was trapped on the container lid. As it touched the lid and cooled, the vapor turned into water again.

PAGE 14 - EGG-SPLOSION

When the water turned from a liquid into a solid, the ice had nowhere to go. The water **expanded** when it froze. This pressure pushed open the egg.

PAGE 16 - MELTING MATTER

The heat inside the oven melted the crayons from a solid to a liquid. As a liquid, they took the shape of the container they were in. When the crayons cooled, they became solid again and formed one large crayon.

PAGE 18 - WHAT'S THE MATTER WITH THIS MATTER?

Adding water to cornstarch creates a mixture. Tiny pieces in the grains of cornstarch lock up and become hard. The molecules made the mixture more like a solid than a liquid.

density—how heavy or light an object is in relation to its size
water vapor—water in gas form
expand—to grow larger

GLOSSARY

balance scale (BA-luhnts SKALE)—an instrument used for weighing things; when two objects are balanced, they weigh the same

condensation (kahn-duhn-SAY-shuhn)—to change from a gas to a liquid

density (DEN-si-tee)—how heavy or light an object is in relation to its size

evaporation (i-vap-uh-RAY-shun)—to change from a liquid to a gas

expand (ik-SPAND)—to grow larger

float (FLOHT)—to rest on water or air

freeze (FREEZ)—to become solid or icy at a very low temperature

gas (GASS)—matter that is not solid or liquid; a gas can move about freely and does not have a definite shape

liquid (LIK-wid)—matter that is wet and can be poured, such as water

matter (MAT-ur)—anything that has weight and takes up space

melt (MELT)—to change from a solid to a liquid

mixture (MIKS-chur)—something made up of different things mixed together

mold (MOHLD)—a model of an object

solid (SOL-id)—matter that holds its shape

water vapor (WAH-tur VAY-pur)—water in gas form

READ MORE

Adler, David A. *Things That Float and Things That Don't.* New York: Holiday House, 2013.

Hughes, Susan. *Does It Sink or Float?* What's the Matter? New York: Crabtree Publishing Company, 2014.

Weakland, Mark. *Bubbles Float, Bubbles Pop.* Science Starts. Mankato, Minn.: Capstone Press, 2011.

INTERNET SITES

FactHound offers a safe, fun way to find Internet sites related to this book. All of the sites on FactHound have been researched by our staff.

Here's all you do:

Visit *www.facthound.com*

Type in this code: 9781491450345

INDEX